YOUR PASSPORT TO

ICELAND

by Nancy Dickmann

CAPSTONE PRESS
a capstone imprint

Published by Capstone Press, an imprint of Capstone
1710 Roe Crest Drive, North Mankato, Minnesota 56003
capstonepub.com

Library of Congress Cataloging-in-Publication Data is available on the Library of Congress website.
ISBN: 9798875245633 (hardcover)
ISBN: 9798875245589 (paperback)
ISBN: 9798875245596 (ebook PDF)

Summary: What is it like to live in or visit Iceland? What makes Iceland's culture unique? Explore the sights and daily lives of Icelanders.

Editorial Credits
Editor: Elaine Duncan; Designer: Sarah Bennett; Media Researcher: Rebekah Hubstenberger; Production Specialist: Tori Abraham

Image Credits
Alamy: IMAGO/Votos - Roland Owsnitzki, 29, SPCOLLECTION, 8; Capstone Press: Eric Gohl, 5; Getty Images: Alexander Scheuber, 14, iStock/Joanne Wastchak, 20, iStock/PEDRE, 12, iStock/tailiwei, 7, iStock/TomasSereda, 16, John Moore, 13, Oleg Breslavtsev, 15, Paul Gilham, 27, Sean Gallup, 18, Sophia Groves, 25, Thomas H. Mitchell, cover, wanderluster, 19; Shutterstock: Drakuliren, 6; Superstock: Image Asset Management/World History Archive, 9, Ragnar Sigurdsson/Arctic-Images, 23

Design Elements
Shutterstock: Flipser, Light-leak Creative, Net Vector, pingebat, topbro

Printed and bound in Malaysia. 006460

CONTENTS

Words in **bold** are in the glossary.

CHAPTER ONE

WELCOME TO ICELAND!

Red-hot **lava** oozes out of the ground. It shoots up into the air. This lava is coming from a crack in the ground. A volcano is erupting! People stand at a safe distance. They watch in awe as the lava flows slowly across the ground. It will cool and turn into hard black rock. This is an active volcano. It's on the Reykjanes Peninsula in Iceland.

Iceland is a small island nation in the north Atlantic Ocean. It lies just south of the **Arctic Circle**. It has cold winters and cool summers. Iceland is part of Europe. Nearly 400,000 people live here. Iceland has many historic sites. It also has natural beauty. Tourists come to see its rugged landscape and beautiful waterfalls.

Explore Iceland's cities and landmarks.

A NORTHERN ISLAND

Iceland has a jagged coastline. It is more than 3,000 miles (4,800 kilometers) long. Steep inlets with cliffs on each side called **fjords** cut into the coast. Iceland has many mountains. There are also beautiful lakes and waterfalls. Much of the land is **tundra**, where the ground is covered with moss and lichen. There are also small areas of forest. Iceland is often windy, and storms are common.

Norse mythology was important to early settlers. Odin was known as the god of knowledge and death.

LAND OF VIKINGS

Iceland was settled by Vikings more than 1,100 years ago. They set up a new life in a harsh land. They had to be tough, and they had to work together. Icelanders are still like this. Iceland has always had a small population for its size. Today, more than 90 percent of its people are native Icelanders. There are a small number of immigrants. They mostly come from Poland and other European countries. Most people in Iceland are Christian. They speak a language called Icelandic. People also learn English and Danish at school.

FACT FILE

OFFICIAL NAME: .... ICELAND

POPULATION: 396,724

LAND AREA: .... 39,769 SQ. MI. (103,000 SQ KM)

CAPITAL: .... REYKJAVIK

MONEY: .... ICELANDIC KRÓNA

GOVERNMENT: .... PARLIAMENTARY REPUBLIC

LANGUAGE: .... ICELANDIC

GEOGRAPHY: Iceland is an island northwest of mainland Europe. It lies between the Greenland Sea and the North Atlantic Ocean. Iceland has many smaller islands surrounding the main island.

NATURAL RESOURCES: Iceland produces a lot of hydroelectric and geothermal power. The main industries are fishing and tourism. It also has aluminum and diatomite.

The Sun Voyager sculpture in Reykjavik represents the quest to find new lands.

CHAPTER TWO

HISTORY OF ICELAND

There are no **Indigenous** people in Iceland. In 325 BCE, a Greek explorer wrote about a northern island that he called "Thule." This might have been Iceland. However, the first permanent settlers didn't arrive until about 874 CE. A Viking from Norway named Ingólfr Arnarson was the first to arrive. He brought his wife and half brother with him. They built a home and farmed the land. They raised sheep and cattle. They grew vegetables. Soon other settlers arrived, mainly from Norway.

Ingólfr Arnarson and other Vikings traveled by boat to Iceland and settled in current day Reykjavik.

CHANGING TIMES

The first Icelandic settlers worshipped Norse gods, such as Thor and Odin. In the late 900s, **missionaries** arrived from Norway. They converted many people to Christianity. In about 1000, a new law was made. Everyone had to become Christian.

Early writers in Iceland wrote down their history. Their stories are called sagas.

In the 1260s, conflict between local chiefs within the country led to its decline. Iceland lost its **independence**. The chiefs still made many of the decisions. But the island was now part of the kingdom of Norway.

FACT

Iceland has one of the world's oldest **parliaments**. It is called the Althing. It was founded in 930 CE. Local chiefs met each summer. They made laws and heard court cases.

LONG ROAD TO FREEDOM

Norway and Denmark joined together in 1380. They became a single kingdom. Iceland was part of it for hundreds of years. But some Icelanders wanted independence. They thought that local people should run the country. In 1904, the Icelandic people got the power to make decisions on local issues.

In World War II (1939–1945), Germany invaded Denmark and took over. But they did not reach Iceland. Both the **Allies** and the **Axis powers** wanted to control Iceland. Its location made it a good place to base ships and planes. The British army invaded Iceland in 1940. One year later, American troops took over. In 1943, the Icelandic people voted not to renew the agreement that made Iceland part of Denmark. Iceland became officially independent in 1944. Sveinn Björnsson was elected as its first president.

MODERN ICELAND

In 1944, Iceland had only about 121,000 people. There were few paved roads and no big cities. Most people farmed or fished for a living. But it soon became more modern.

TIMELINE OF ICELANDIC HISTORY

ABOUT 874 CE: The first settlers arrive in Iceland from Norway.

930 CE: A parliament called the Althing is set up. It still exists today.

ABOUT 1000: By 1000, all Icelanders are officially Christian.

1264: Iceland becomes part of the kingdom of Norway.

1380: Norway and Denmark join to form a single kingdom.

1494–95: A plague kills about half the population of Iceland.

1904: Iceland gets the power to run its own parliament.

1940: Germany occupies Denmark, and British forces occupy Iceland.

1944: Iceland becomes independent.

1949: Iceland becomes one of the founding members of NATO.

1980: Vigdís Finnbogadóttir of Iceland becomes the world's first female head of state.

2008: A financial crisis collapses the Icelandic economy.

Factories, power plants, and roads were built. Fishermen were able to freeze their catch. Then they could export it. Iceland traded its fish for goods from other countries. Iceland became one of the founding countries of the North Atlantic Treaty Organization (NATO) in 1949. This group of countries work to help and protect each other.

In 2008, risky banking decisions led to Iceland's financial crisis. Three major Icelandic banks failed. It took several years for the economy to recover.

CHAPTER THREE

EXPLORE ICELAND

More than 2 million people visit Iceland every year. Many of them come for its natural beauty. Iceland's location is unique. It is a place where the Earth's crust is pulling apart. This causes cracks in the ground. Hot lava can seep out. This is how Iceland's volcanoes formed. When lava cools, it forms rock called basalt. Iceland's entire surface is volcanic rock. There are more than 100 volcanoes. Between 30 and 40 are considered active.

Basalt columns at the Aldeyjarfoss waterfall in northern Iceland

The Sundhnúkur volcano erupted in the Reykjanes Peninsula on June 2, 2024, near Grindavik, Iceland.

ERUPTIONS

Volcanic eruptions are common in Iceland. Some come from cone-shaped volcanoes such as Hekla. Others come from cracks in the ground. But a volcano can remain quiet, or dormant, for years. People visit when it is safe. They can hike to the top of volcanoes such as Askja. There is a lake in its crater. The trail is about 8 miles (13 km) long. Tourists also explore lava fields. There are amazing shapes in the cooled lava.

FACT

Thingvellir is a national park. It lies along the line where the Earth's crust is pulling apart. There are steep cliffs with deep canyons between them. Earthquakes occur often here.

ICE AND WATER

Parts of Iceland are covered by glaciers. They are like rivers of ice. They move very slowly. Beneath some there are stunning ice caves. These caves are carved out by melted water from glaciers. Iceland is also famous for waterfalls. There are more than 10,000! The water comes from melted snow and glaciers. It falls over steep drops in the mountains. On the coast there are fjords. They were once valleys carved by glaciers. Then they filled with water.

The Seljalandsfoss waterfall is about 200 feet (60 meters) tall.

ANCIENT HOMES

Iceland does not have many trees. Early settlers couldn't build wooden homes. Instead, they used stone and turf. People built houses from volcanic stone. Then they made the roofs from turf. Turf is a thick mat of grass and soil. This kept the house warm. Some of these houses have been preserved. People can visit and even sleep in them!

THE BLUE LAGOON

In Iceland, melted rock called **magma** makes it very hot underground. There are many natural hot springs. The Blue Lagoon is a famous bathing pool. It was opened as a bathing facility in 1987. It is filled with naturally heated water from underground. People come to bathe in its milky blue waters. The water gets its color from the minerals it contains. Even if it is cold and snowy, the water is warm. It stays between 98 and 104 degrees Fahrenheit (37 and 40 degrees Celsius).

REYKJAVIK

Reykjavik is Iceland's capital. It is also the largest city. About two-thirds of the country's people live there. Many of the buildings are modern. They are heated by hot water from underground. So are many outdoor swimming pools. Reykjavik has shops, cafés, museums, and theaters.

The Hallgrimskirkja church in Reykjavik was opened in 1986. It is the second tallest building in Iceland.

SMALLER TOWNS

Akureyri is the second largest city in Iceland. It is on the north coast surrounded by mountains. Many tourists come in the winter to ski. The town is an important fishing port.

Hafnarfjordur is southwest of Reykjavik. It has quaint houses and a beautiful botanic garden. Every summer it hosts a Viking festival. People set up a Viking market. There, they sell leather, furs, silver jewelry, and carved horns. People in costumes stage fake battles.

FACT

Most towns in Iceland are near the coast. One long, circular road called the "Ring Road" connects them. It is more than 800 miles (1,287 km) long. People often drive the whole route. They stop to explore along the way.

CHAPTER FOUR

DAILY LIFE

Iceland has changed a lot. One hundred years ago, most people lived on farms or in small villages. Now, more than 94 percent of people live in urban areas. They live in houses and apartments. They get around by car, bus, or bike. But history and tradition are still very important to Icelanders. Many people still work in the fishing industry. Others help tourists by working in hotels and restaurants.

Atlantic cod, pollack, and haddock are some of the most common fish found in the waters surrounding Iceland.

Education in Iceland is free, even day care and preschool. College is also free. Iceland has seven universities. It has more women in the workforce than most other countries in Europe. Iceland was also the first country where companies must prove that they pay women the same as men.

LANGUAGE

The Icelandic language is old. It is close to how the Vikings once spoke. To come up with a name for new inventions, a committee invents a new word. For example, the word for telephone comes from older words meaning "long thread." The word for helicopter means "twirling rush."

Icelanders proudly wear sweaters made in a traditional pattern. The wool from local sheep keeps them warm.

FOOD AND DRINK

Iceland's early settlers had to eat what they could find. They used local resources such as fish. They raised sheep for meat and milk. Fish and milk are still a core part of the Icelandic menu. But now other ingredients are imported. Heated greenhouses grow a range of fruits and vegetables. Immigrants from places such as Asia have brought their own dishes.

POPULAR DISHES

Fish is one of the main foods. People eat it fresh, smoked, or dried. They make it into stews. People also eat lamb. A dish called hangikjot is often served at Christmas. It's made of lamb that is smoked and then boiled. Icelanders also eat skyr. This soft cheese is a little like yogurt. It is made from cow's milk.

Icelanders eat a dark, dense bread called rugbraud. It is made from rye.

PÖNNUKÖKUR

Thin pancakes are a popular dessert in Iceland. They are cooked in a flat, heavy pan that never gets washed. People pass these pans down from one generation to the next.

Ingredients

- 2 ½ cups all-purpose flour
- ½ teaspoon baking powder
- pinch of salt
- 2 cups milk
- 2 eggs
- 2 tablespoons vanilla
- 3 tablespoons butter
- Sugar, berries, whipped cream, or toppings of your choice

Directions

1. Mix the flour, baking powder, and salt in a large bowl.
2. Add half the milk and whisk until smooth.
3. Whisk in the eggs, then add the rest of the milk and the vanilla. Mix well.
4. Ask an adult to help you melt the butter. Use a large, flat pan over medium heat. Pour some of the melted butter into the batter, leaving a thin coating in the pan.
5. Use a ladle to pour batter into the middle of the pan. Use enough to make a thin layer.
6. After a minute or so, carefully slide a spatula under the edge, and flip it over to cook the other side.
7. Put the pancake on a plate and fold it into quarters. You can sprinkle it with sugar or put berries and whipped cream on top. Rhubarb jam and skyr are traditional toppings.

CHAPTER FIVE

HOLIDAYS AND CELEBRATIONS

Christian holidays such as Easter are important in Iceland. Before the start of Lent on Ash Wednesday there are two days of fun. On Monday, "Bun Day," people eat pastries filled with whipped cream. On Tuesday, "Bursting Day," they eat a special lamb stew. When Easter comes, families share a meal of roast lamb. People give each other chocolate eggs.

CHRISTMAS

Christmas is another popular holiday. Since this time of year is cold and dark in Iceland, people hang lights. Icelandic legend tells of 13 brothers called "Yule Lads." In stories, they pull pranks and cause mischief. Starting on December 12, one visits every night. They put presents in shoes left on the windowsill. On Christmas Day, families share a meal. They watch movies and play games.

People shop for gifts at outdoor markets. The markets also sell hot food and drinks.

FACT

Books and reading are an important part of Icelandic culture. At Christmas, it is traditional to give books as gifts. Most people open their gifts on Christmas Eve. Then they can read them with a cup of hot cocoa!

CELEBRATING HISTORY AND SEASONS

People in Iceland celebrate their independence on June 17. There are parades and dancing. Icelanders also celebrate the seasons. They have parties to mark the first day of summer, which is the Thursday after April 18. People celebrate the summer solstice on June 21. This is the longest day of the year. In autumn, farmers round up sheep and horses for the winter. This is an old tradition. Hard work is followed by singing and dancing.

ONLY IN ICELAND

Icelanders love to celebrate their unique culture. Thorrablot comes in late January and early February. It is based on old Viking feasts to honor the gods. People gather to eat traditional food. They sing and recite poetry. In August, the town of Hafnarfjordur hosts a "hidden people festival." This celebrates elves, which many Icelanders believe in.

Icelanders celebrate Pride in August. Reykjavik is full of rainbows to show support for the LGBTQ+ community.

CHAPTER SIX

SPORTS AND RECREATION

Soccer is the most popular sport in Iceland. Many people play for fun. There are also professional teams. Even though Iceland is a small country, its national teams do well. Both the men's and women's teams have played in the European Championships. The men's team also played in the World Cup.

Handball is also very popular. This indoor game is fast-paced. Teams work to throw a ball into the goal. Iceland's handball team won a silver medal at the 2008 Olympics.

Glíma is a style of Icelandic wrestling. It dates back to the Viking times. People still compete today. Icelanders are also famous for their success in strongman competitions. They compete in weight lifting and strength contests.

Icelanders cheer for the national soccer team by doing the "Viking Clap."

HUNDABEIN

This game's name means "dog bones." It's played by two teams that can be any size. The number of players must be the same on each team. One person stays out to be the leader.

What You Need:

- two teams with an equal amount of players
- a leader
- a dog bone (a medium-sized object such as a beanbag or a ball)

What You Do:

1. Split into two teams. The players on each team get a number, starting with 1.
2. Each team stands along a line, facing each other. The lines should be about 60 feet (18 m) apart.
3. The leader puts a dog bone (or other object) in the middle. Then they call out a number.
4. The two players with that number race to grab the bone. The one that gets it runs back to their line. The other player tries to tag them.
5. If the player makes it back safely, their team gets a point. If they get tagged, the other team gets the point.
6. The players line up again, and the leader calls a new number.

ARTS AND CULTURE

The arts are very important in Iceland. Creativity is encouraged from an early age. A tradition of storytelling goes back to the Viking days. People would gather around the fire to listen to thrilling stories. Today, there are many authors in Iceland. Reykjavik hosts bookfairs and festivals.

Hildur Guðnadóttir plays the cello and writes music for films. She is the first Icelander to win an Oscar.

Folk music was once performed across Iceland. Some people still play it. Other musicians today perform modern music. The singer Björk and the band Sigur Rós are both from Iceland. They are popular around the world.

SOMETHING FOR EVERYONE

Iceland is small but beautiful. It has stunning scenery and a unique culture. Its people have kept the culture of their Viking ancestors alive. And they have given it a modern twist! From volcanoes to glaciers, cities to villages, there is something for everyone to enjoy.

GLOSSARY

Allies (AL-lyz)
the countries that fought against Germany in World War II (1939–1945), including the United States, United Kingdom, and Soviet Union

Arctic Circle (ARK-tik SUR-kuhl)
an imaginary line encircling an area around the North Pole, where it is cold all year round

Axis powers (ACK-sis POW-uhrz)
a group of countries that fought together in World War II, including Japan, Italy, and Germany

fjord (fee-ORD)
a long, narrow inlet of ocean between high cliffs

independence (in-di-PEN-duhns)
freedom from the control of other people or things

Indigenous (in-DI-juh-nuhs)
the original inhabitants of a certain place

lava (LAH-vuh)
the hot, liquid rock that pours out of a volcano when it erupts

magma (MAG-muh)
melted rock found under the Earth's surface

missionary (MISH-uh-nair-ee)
a person who works on behalf of a religious group to spread the group's faith

parliament (PAHR-luh-muhnt)
a group of people who make laws and run the government in some countries

tundra (TUHN-druh)
a cold area where trees do not grow; the soil under the ground in the tundra is permanently frozen.

READ MORE

Leatherland, Noah. *Life in the Viking Age.* Minneapolis: Bearport Publishing, 2025.

Murray, Julie. *Famous Volcanoes*. Minneapolis: Abdo Books, 2022.

Ólafsdóttir, Linda. *I Dare! I Can! I Will!: The Day the Icelandic Women Walked Out and Inspired the World.* Petaluma, CA: Cameron Kids, 2023.

INTERNET SITES

Britannica Kids: Iceland
kids.britannica.com/students/article/Iceland/275026

History for Kids: The Vikings: Facts & Information for Kids
historyforkids.org/the-vikings-facts-for-kids

National Geographic Kids: Iceland
kids.nationalgeographic.com/geography/countries/article/iceland

INDEX

ABOUT THE AUTHOR

Nancy Dickmann grew up in the United States before moving to England, where she worked as a children's book editor. She now has her dream job as a full-time author and has written more than 250 books for children, mainly on science topics. Her favorite part of the job is researching and learning new things. One highlight was getting to interview a real astronaut to find out about using the toilet in space!

SELECT BOOKS IN THIS SERIES

YOUR PASSPORT TO AUSTRALIA
YOUR PASSPORT TO BRAZIL
YOUR PASSPORT TO CUBA
YOUR PASSPORT TO EGYPT
YOUR PASSPORT TO ENGLAND
YOUR PASSPORT TO GERMANY
YOUR PASSPORT TO JAPAN
YOUR PASSPORT TO MEXICO
YOUR PASSPORT TO PORTUGAL
YOUR PASSPORT TO SAUDI ARABIA